THIS WALKER BOOK BELONGS TO:

_____

_____

_____

_____

Guess where I live

illustrated by **Anni Axworthy**

WALKER BOOKS
AND SUBSIDIARIES
LONDON · BOSTON · SYDNEY

Where do I live?

This is me.
I'm a monkey.

hot
e

It rains
nearly
every day.

arrots
too.

hot
e

It rains
nearly
every day.

arrots
too.

My home is hot and there are lots of trees.

It rains nearly every day.

Snakes and parrots live here, too.

Jungles are also called rainforests.

Where do I live?

This is me. I'm a Polar bear.

My home is cold and snowy.

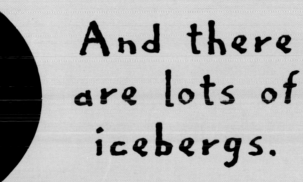

And there are lots of icebergs.

Seals and foxes live here, too.

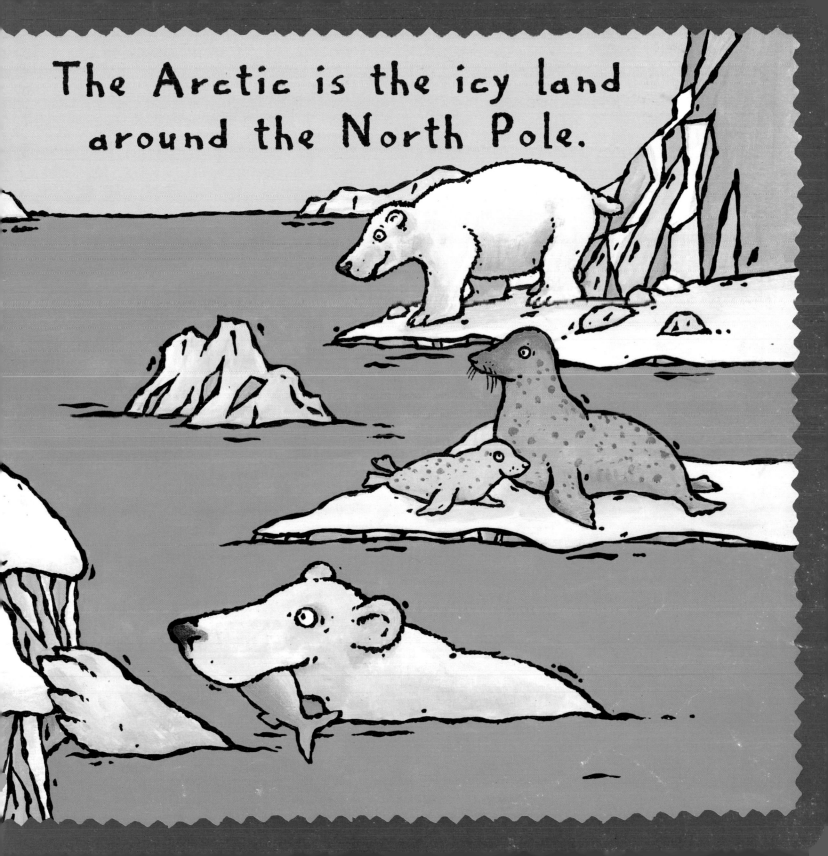

The Arctic is the icy land around the North Pole.

My home is
under water.

There are
lots of rocks
and seaweed.

Starfish and limpets
live here, too.

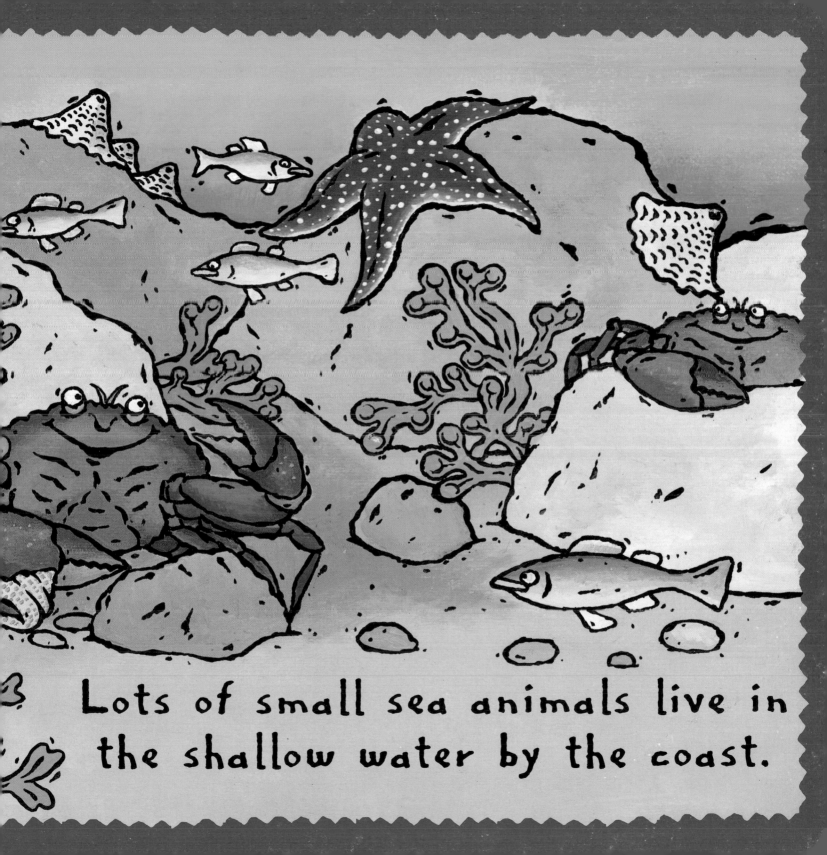

Lots of small sea animals live in the shallow water by the coast.

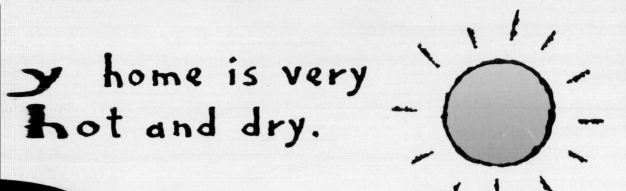

y home is very hot and dry.

There are lots of sandy hills.

zards and scorpions live here, too.

My home is very
hot and dry.

There are lots
of sandy hills.

Lizards and scorpions
live here, too.

Deserts are places where it hardly ever rains.

Where do I live?

This is me.
I'm a Golden
eagle.

My home is rocky and high up.

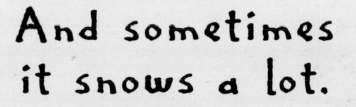

And sometimes it snows a lot.

Goats and hares live here, too.

On the top of high
mountains the snow
never melts.

We're in the wrong homes! Can you remember where we really live?

First published 1999 by Walker Books Ltd
87 Vauxhall Walk, London SE11 5HJ

This edition published 2000

2 4 6 8 10 9 7 5 3 1

Series concept and design by Louise Jackson

Words by Louise Jackson and Paul Harrison

Wildlife consultant: Martin Jenkins

This book has been typeset in Joe Overweight.

Printed in Singapore

British Library Cataloguing in Publication Data
A catalogue record for this book is available
from the British Library.

ISBN 0-7445-7745-4